ECLIPSE ON JOYPITER

notionpress
.com

ECLIPSE ON JOYPITER

Pritika Rao

notionpress.com

Notion Press

Old No. 38, New No. 6

McNichols Road, Chetpet

Chennai - 600 031

First Published by Notion Press 2015

ISBN 978-93-5206-410-6

Cover art: Sanjana Rebecca

Other illustrations: Mala Sen

For G. Joseph, Samuel Rao and P.S.S Rao;
The combustion triangle that sets my heart on fire and keeps me burning bright

Preface

Unlike his popular, hot-headed blazing cousin from whom you have to shield your eyes, there is the solitary moon, with the faint tinge of cheesy glow in the night sky, a handsome companion to the darkness with his cheeky hide-and-seek peeking, charmingly teasing out a relationship with the shadows.

The whole earth is in incessant transformation. We have all experienced the wondrous misfortune of loss. Even this hypnotising marker in the sky, our hero on a lonely cyclic journey, is temporarily obscured by the shadows. Questions hang in the sky like stars, curiosity suffocates you like a thick blanket and though physically there is the death of either a relationship or a person, Hope can survive as a dangerously immortal being. It is during this period; when love of astronomical proportion is cloaked by the dull fogginess of the passing of a soul; When there's a storm in heaven and reasoning falls flat; When intelligence and truth can do little to prevent the dark fingers of pain from casting mocking shadows and encroaching upon your once-radiant identity. This is the core from which the new things are born. Like a crumpled embryo in the pit of watery black, life begins to take form. For me, that period birthed these words.

The book is divided into three parts; beginning with the primping of hope and longing, then transitioning into the dimness of impending defeat and culminating in profound loss. These are intended to mirror the chaos of souring love in the stages of an eclipse. Some of these poems were birthed in retrospect, a few in the heat of the moment, and others in the cool of the rain.

I write these words for the broken-hearted, the ones who dwell in the deepest umbra, for those who are wondering if there is anything that can help you scrub the coal of the night off your skin. When you try desperately to fit your broken life in a box and tearfully wrap your loose ends, there is one promise you can hold on to and one that I hope you will wholly embrace: You will make it through the night and joy will find you in the morning[1].

He appointed the moon for seasons: the sun knoweth his going down.

Psalm 104:19, The Bible (King James Version)

ACKNOWLEDGEMENTS

Without these fabulous people, these poems would have gathered dust in a small corner of the internet or the margins of an old notebook. I am deeply indebted to you all:

Mama, the core of my heart, loudest cheerleader and encourager of my dreams; you are not just the reason I am alive but my inspiration to live fully, fearlessly and joyfully.

Samu, my hero; you always have my back and allow me to be brave.

Dada, my backbone; for the inheritance of your love of literature, your constant support & the editing and proof-reading of this book.

Mala Sen, your passionate critique and positive reinforcement were the driving force behind the creative process of this book. Thank you for your generosity, honesty and wonderful illustrations.

Sanjana Rebecca, for your lovely work and for stepping in so graciously when I needed you.

Zubin Jehangir, thank you for telling me to do this and believing that I could.

Abishek, Nina, Radhika and Debarati; for unwearyingly entertaining all my silly obsessions, fears and hesitations and reinforcing the confidence & determination I needed to complete this book.

Nivedita Raju, for your invaluable advice.

Thanks to the entire Notion Press team for your patience, expert guidance, and faith in this book.

Most importantly, the Maker of my soul; You plant the seeds and cause them to bloom. I am blessed because You so lovingly make all my wildest dreams come true. You are the love of my life. In everything I do, may all glory be Yours.

Contents

UMBRA

Antumbra

Derived from the Latin ante for 'before and umbra 'shadow', the antumbra is the region from which the occluding body appears entirely contained within the disc of the light source. An observer in this region experiences an annular eclipse, in which a bright ring is visible around the eclipsing body. If the observer moves closer to the light source, the apparent size of the occluding body increases until it causes a full umbra.[2]

Chasing Grace

Sweet summer sun fades to butter moon night
Sparkling heavens birthed from eventide
Are the trees alive with a magic of sorts?
Do they hear your voice, your silent thoughts?
Unfurling wind carries old forgotten words
Echoes resounding cryptic songs of birds
I breathe deep and follow with lingering hope
Feet tapping on earth floor stones, with outstretched arms I grope
The ground gives way; I crumble, into the earth I sink
As rotating world steadies slow beneath starlight's wink.
The ache of the fall cripples the rise
Panic briefly grips my throat as worry writhes
A backdrop of silence falls dark as blackened coal
As the dirt beneath my feet marks my sin spattered soul
But when the flames of the galaxy catch the light in my eyes,
My heart sees your face and opens wide to the grace of the skies.

Eidyllio

In the midst of heavy conversation
and muggy June heat,
distinguished company and
rhythmic beat.
With a girl on each arm,
And a third on the horizon
I see you in the distance
this is clearly your best season
As you part the crowd,
the space between us evaporates
and my head grows faint
as your arms frame my waist.
Summer's love affairs
are hardest to erase
sunshine warms the heart
and dries the mind to a haze.
All order gives way to chaos
and now, guilt is awake
but we've gone too far
to interrupt this mistake.
As all good things do,
this will come to an end
and we weave tangled webs

for the future to mend.
We used to dance on rainbows
our days were long
we were pretty as a picture,
romantic as a song.
My mind's printed image
of us is a dream
they say the truth sets you free
but it's not what it seems.
For a love like ours
we can't parade like some
memories of that time
I'll keep 'til kingdom come.
And when I am questioned,
although I may deny;
my heart will still whisper
a silent love sigh.

Circus

I was inspired by Solomon,
when he spoke of gazelle and doe
and insisted that we wait for love.
But discipline, it evaded me so.
We'd like to think of ourselves as trapeze artists
in this circus of love-
Mad enough to jump
without someone to catch and twirl you.
A magnificent show! Ah, the magical thrill!
Worth the risk you say? Then maybe I will.
So, I prowled the streets for you
in most un-ladylike fashion,
singing and dancing, blurting truths with burning cheek
In frequent glassy-eyed episodes.
Do we ever really learn?
Ever really recover?
Ever really see?
That without someone to catch you
in this circus of love:
We trapeze artists
are foolishly falling, endlessly.

Flying Penguins

I point to the sky one afternoon
See geese flying in a V
Gee, I think aloud
that must certainly be lucky!
O time traveller, where have you gone?
Quick! Lend me your time machine
I must travel afar and
The maps on my wall are torn down!
Yes, I've tried everything
If he were here, I'd tell him too
Fairytales are for children, I know
And we're much too fancy for that
But I wish you'd left me crumbs in the mud
So I could have followed them to you.
No journey is too difficult
Not if your pursuit true
When penguins fly and
Elephants dance ballet
That day, I'll be with you
Too fantastic are these dreams
For a lone thinker like me
Madness, they say, can she not see

What's plain-as-nose reality?
I would tell them what I kept hidden
In a box beneath my bed,
In my heart and in my head:
If dreaming in moon's company is quite alright
Could it hurt to be whimsical in daylight?

Journey

In deepest dark and deafening quiet
two lonely lights pass in the night
with iron will as captain,
a cloudy eyed journey
with vision torn by rain.
we don't cross each other often
and these days are city stars
but tonight, under yellow moon
this is our last chance.
Home is a safe place separated from here by miles
and many a metal heart
so drop your anchor,
stay a while?
behind this curtain of black,
nobody will us find
when daylight falls we must be gone
but until then,
and for now, we are one.

Luminary Lovers

Luminary lovers,
Your eyes clear as crystal
Conceal heavy hearts of gold
In time, blazing fiery world will stare you down
And grip your heart, fighting to take hold
'Don't look away', I plead.
Look right at me, for these hours are numbered
Quiet will return, darkness clothe us again
Nobody else this much I need.
Luminary lovers,
Be not disheartened in the waning
Bring not the blinds down upon your soul
Remember your time together in solitary sky
Patience, the only road to that goal
'Together', you reply steady
And I breathe these words, familiar and deep
Ready to take flight
"This isn't my home", I whisper giddy as I gaze below
As our fingers interlace and toes grow light.

Sea Princess

It's exhausting yet mine;

A life, aquatic

Every day trying to keep your head

Above water.

As the gentle waves wash over your horizon.

Constantly swimming,

Yet bound to the sea

Only to get as far as the shore.

Would I be to you a treasure as a chest or a pearl?

Maybe no more than a 'catch of the day'

Numbered with tropical fish and crustaceans

I see mountains

I never can climb

A field of grass

Only my water will find

In the silver, coral, icy water

Beneath glistening sun

Plumb the ocean depth and discover me-

a princess of the sea

It's exhausting yet familiar

a life, aquatic

every day working to stay afloat

Perhaps our lives are just the same

aren't we all trying to keep the salt from our throats?

Penumbra

Derived *from* the latin paene *for* 'almost' and umbra 'shadow', the penumbra is a partial shadow, as in an eclipse, between regions of complete shadow and complete illumination. Also refers to an area in which something exists to a lesser or uncertain degree.[3]

Seasoned

If I could rewind to early May
when a promise hung in the damp wind
as expectation turned the corners of the earth
Into concave surrender.
I can see that I lingered too long,
Witnessed your love evaporating
In exhausting summer
You see through me now
My blue sky permanence
Setting light to everything else
Content to lie suffocated behind the clouds
What might have been?
If I were a sparrow
a pigeon
an airplane
Better yet the moon
Wanderer, silent spectator
to your quiet thumping existence
glowing against blackened canopy
would you see me then?

Without a finger to your lips
or shielding your eyes?
Alas, swelling hope bursts into August vain
Squelched in the beating down of monsoon
While the world groans limp with me in pain.

Night Fox

From behind tall trees rises lonely speckled moon
and we stand for a while, but then you run
like a fox in the night.
If only you wouldn't call out to me!
After all would it be wise
to offer alcohol to the faint?
Instinct, that's all I've got.
Since talking to myself
is not what it used to be.
That's crazy, they say!
Oh dear she's doing it again
get on your knees and pray.
Puppets were a rare novelty
now they're everywhere, aren't they?
Oh but it's nice to see you here again!
Like a miracle on a messy day
we are all a little dusty
on the whole romance front.
I see the line, yet willingly, I stray
Preserving guilt in pixel font
I write what my mouth dare not say:

Could I defy all logic, lay aside all sense
run with you into the unknown
and fit right into your life
as if I never left?

Love and Physics

Measure me time
as clock hands slowly circle
is it television black and white?
Moving earth into dark or light?
Measure me distance
should I break out the compass
walk under bridges broken,
perhaps over distant mountain
or search for direction from within?
If you are so far away from me
but time hasn't moved at all and
if speed is distance over time
will you be quickly mine?

Town Square

Each time,
The same town square
The walls are yellow
Wearing down
Every day an identical route
As I struggle to understand the truth
A paler time there never was
Clouds hang over us, ready to pour
The fight is in the air
At the centre of the old town square.
So many people walk around us
Holding hands, blowing kisses, blushing red
We sit in silence, never meeting each other's eyes
Floundering in the words we never said
I wish you wouldn't meet me here
Yet, we both know this is home
I ask you to stay a while
But you walk away, we're torn.
There is nothing to be earned here
Still, nowhere I would rather be
You may be free, but I'm bound there
Waiting at the entrance to the old town square.

Poison Ivy

You told me we were different
When you told me not to hide
But when hearts were torn open
You turned away as I cried
I waited long, and I waited well
As you sauntered in through the good times
Watched smug each time that I fell
Then you call me poison ivy
And all cords are untied
Though the leaves are freshly watered
Our roots have all run dry.

Movement

There are clues everywhere.
In gurgling laughter marked with dimples
and lines, entwined fingers and
the flutter of little yellow wings
Runs a flowing, deep rhythm of things.
There are so many ways
I could try to fit in
To go with the flow,
Or embrace it all on a whim
But the world it seems has lost its charm
I am movement and noise and everything they say I should be
And if everything that has breath has life
that's what they say, anyway
Then, darling, what has become of me?

Us Against the World

The days roll out before me
And I know a storm is coming
I want you to hold me to your chest
I'm so tired of running.
The air is swirling
Clouds threatening rain
No prayers to prophets,
I've been calling out your name.
We could weather this storm together
You know that to be true
All that's keeping me from dying
Is this enduring hope for you
It's us against the world, love.
You're the armour I need for this fight
That is how I will learn to be brave
The only way I'll get out of this alive.

Traded Dreams

When dreams were placed upon the shelf
we chose right, we did good
we took the ones we knew we should:
of heavenly love, boxes of happiness
carefully ignored the stuff composed of distress
Then we met the world and it spun us tales
visions of power and glory, and all things that shone.
And barter we did, we were thrilled with the steal
until we were stuck at the raw end of the deal.
Now as dreams are realized: life in richly stacked mud
in the claustrophobia of fat wads of paper
of terrified hearts, bubbling corrupt blood
where love is commodity,
pale and sedentary.
Joy is rehearsed theatrical melody
Hell, all emotions mere parody:
This race to success is overrated at best
but the stranger the demon,
the harder the test.
We've traded dreams with the devil
as God looks on mourning our loss
to see angel after angel
choose the fire's gloss.

Umbra

From the latin word meaning 'shadow', the umbra is a dark area, especially the blackest part of a shadow from which all light is cut off.[4]

October

I stand right in the fault lines
Everything displaced but I cannot move
I tell myself to be brave, but I don't even dare blink
The tremors are still murmuring
From that earthquake of hurt.
And I long for October,
For a time before this tumbled world
With all of it shards and shambles,
Love's labour truly lost
The slipping of a heart that in turn tips the will
And a familiar caution fits right in.
The bricks we threw at already dented souls
Had we saved them for mending, we could now rest indoors.
As a lone burning ember leaf falls,
I feel your warm arms around me.
How I wish they were real!
And here I go again
Foolishly longing for October,
When I was your girl.

Never Lost

No room *for* colour
Just your vague *frame*
You can't run *far* it will *follow* you
Doesn't need to know your name
You wait patiently *for* day
But then the stealthy night returns
Sinking sun in purple sky
Say hello to your shadows
Make what you want *of* it but
Remember it grows *from* your toes.

Fall from Grace

Fight still surged through her blood
when they bound her waxy arms
and taped her ruby lips
her weapons did not exude now
their customary charms.
She played with courage
and now feared herself,
bathed in dirt and blood
in miserable health
she lived months of silence
fed on morsels of guilt
wishing she could take it back
dreaming of the life she may have built
On a stone floor- cold as ice
with the cawing of crows
in the company of mice
she carved apologies, letters to her lover
the one who lay as cold as she
deep in the ground, gone forever
She wrote every day until the very end
when she ascended those wooden steps
and her feet would never meet earth again
she didn't lift her eyes

to scan the crowd
what if someone familiar she spied?
Truth be told they probably
wouldn't recognize her face
to no one in particular; she spoke for
the first time in months
'My parents', she said, 'they named me Grace'.

Wallflower

The cobblestone leaks poverty, infecting the road
As she hides in the shadows, maintaining her load
You walk right on by, under sweet shade of your umbrella
She whimpers and you dust it off, make believe you didn't hear her
A charming young lover with a damsel on hand,
Why would you make room for kind sympathy, lad?
Still her bullet gaze bores holes in your steely indifference
But you march straight ahead, taking soldier stance
What are you afraid of? What do you hold to your chest?
That you would stand out, the subject of ridicule and humour at best?
Rain drops easy down the noses of lofty window courtroom
As in these village crevices, more neglected wallflowers bloom.

Surrender

There is much to forget
you wouldn't know
Cloudy reason fogs your mind
you, who proudly believe in no regret
This grief that swallows a soul
and spits it out unrecognizable
an unfair barter
for choosing your heart
and sealing your broken places whole
Alas, there is no hope of return
Give it up, wishful thinking, stubborn will
You blew us up in unforgiving smoke
And left me helpless, holding the gun

THE UNSAID

I wish for cold nights
Just to stick my feet under yours
And be painted with the tender brush of your lips
It splits me down the middle
This amnesia of your heart
Every inch of me is aching
From the lashing of your whips
Things unsaid hang over us like a cloud
withholding sweet rain
As the days rumble along without end
And I try weakly to harvest
In this famine of pain
The many things I couldn't say
Could I write them to you now
The regrets in ghostly whispers
and fears in verse, but most importantly
the weight of my love,
Could I leave them here without making a sound?
They sit there,
right raw at the tip of my tongue
The things I cannot seem to swallow
Everything that can't be undone
The words I should have said
That will now never see the sun.

Wounds

I call you by name
Give you sweet core of my heart
Dance in delusion that we
Never could part
Speak not of the devil
Don't even think it true
All your worst fears
In vulnerability will burn through
Look at you now,
Glowing indifference
Broken bridges give way
Destroying pretence
"What's done is done!"
You blurt, blunt and raw
Cutting right to my soul
The depth of which
You never saw.

Proof

You lit a match and left me burning
Was it really as easy as that?
Took a lazy stroll and won't be returning
How do I win you back?
You say earnestly that you loved me
And maybe still do
But your eyes give it away, all stony red
And I know these words are easier said,
You see my love is still here
as firm as when you left
You need look no further
than the tears that I have shed
Although I am no fortune-teller
I know what will happen now
You will swear you love me
But I hear the flat lining
And baby, we are dead.

Empty Cups

In the final wisps of winter
Between puffs of cigarette smoke cloud
You are unrecognizable when you utter goodbye
And I lose you to the crowd.

I spend days twirling the words around
They, like bubbling lather, rise
As I cough up reluctant breath
And try to trace a way back to you, following breadcrumbs of lies

Sooner or later sunshine creeps in shy
Pricking the tips of my fingers,
Teasing out the familiar creases and ridges
Where your warm touch once notoriously lingered.

Each time to this diluted pool of memories-
I return, unconscious and scooped hollow by grief.
Then it churns again; this liquid lava in my heart, brimming crescent eyes
A dangerous pattern I'd be wise not to keep.

The cure lies not in perspective:
For whether half full or empty,
Reasoning combusts like stars
When hungry love defeats philosophy.

Phantom

In a big bowl of white China

There is a soup of nothingness

I'm drinking eager, repeatedly

In desperate attempt to cure this mess

A gaping hole in the canvas of my being

Vast fabric of cords and emblems that signify

A relationship eroded lean

I long for some roborant to ease this pain

As with any severed body part

Without you

Inky blue gathers thick and stale

Like lost blood on gauze

And all I have left are these words

Laying it all out: what could have been,

And once was.

References

1. Paraphrased *from* Psalm 30:5, The Bible, King James Version

2. http://en.wikipedia.org/wiki/Umbra,_penumbra_and _antumbra#Antumbra

3. penumbra. (n.d.) American Heritage® Dictionary *of* the English Language, Fifth Edition. (2011). Retrieved May 6 2015 *from* http://www.thefreedictionary.com/penumbra

4. umbra. (n.d.) American Heritage® Dictionary *of* the English Language, Fifth Edition. (2011). Retrieved May 6 2015 *from* http://www.thefreedictionary.com/umbra